FOOD

BREAD

Jillian Powell

WAYLAND

Titles in the series

BREAD   EGGS   FISH   FRUIT
MILK   PASTA   POTATOES
POULTRY   RICE   VEGETABLES

First published in 1996 by Wayland (Publishers) Ltd
61 Western Road, Hove, East Sussex, BN3 1JD, England

© 1996 Wayland (Publishers) Ltd

Series Editor: Sarah Doughty
Editor: Liz Harman
Design: Jean Wheeler
Illustration: Peter Bull
Cover: Zul Mukhida, Chapel Studios; photostylist Liz Miller

British Library Cataloguing in Publication Data
Powell, Jillian
Bread. – (Food)
1. Bread – Juvenile literature
2. Cookery (Bread) – Juvenile literature
I. Title
641.8'15

ISBN 0 7502 1796 0

Typeset by Jean Wheeler

Printed and bound in Italy by L.E.G.O. S.p.A., Vicenza

Title page picture: A bread stall at the busy market at Damascas Gate in Israel.

Picture acknowledgements

Cephas 6 (top), 12 (both), 14 (bottom), 16 (top), 17 (both), 18 (bottom), 21 (top), 22 (bottom), 24 (bottom); Chapel Studios 4 (top), 10 (top), 11 (both), 14 (top), 15, 16 (bottom), 18–19 (top), 19 (bottom); James Davis Travel Photography title page, 13 (top); Mary Evans 8, 9; Eye Ubiquitous contents page, 5, 13 (bottom), 21 (bottom); Michael Holford 6 (bottom), 7; Hutchison Library 23 (top); Life File 22 (top), 24 (top); Christine Osborne 23 (bottom); Edward Parker 4 (bottom), 10 (bottom), 20; South American Pictures 25 (both).

Contents

An ancient food 4
How bread began 6
Bread in the past 8
What is in bread? 10
How bread is made 12
The food in bread 14
How we eat bread 16
Bread in Europe 18
Bread around the world 20
Bread and religion 22
Festivals and customs 24
Bread recipes for you to try 26
Glossary 30
Books to read 31
Index 32

An ancient food

◀ A selection of bread from around the world, including: nan, tortillas, chapatis, a baguette, rye bread, soda bread, crumpets and pitta bread.

Bread dough is made with flour. Flour can be made from ground cereal grains like wheat, barley or rye or from dried and grated starchy vegetables like potatoes or cassava. In Europe and the USA, bread dough is usually mixed with a leaven, such as yeast, sourdough or buttermilk, to make the bread rise. In India, the Middle East and Mexico flat, unleavened bread is made.

▼ This woman in Brazil is making flat bread, using flour ground from cassava, a type of root vegetable. Cassava bread is an important part of the daily diet for people living in Amazonia.

Bread is one of our oldest foods. In many countries, it is eaten with every meal of the day, and it is an important part of religious ceremonies and festivals. There are hundreds of different kinds of bread, from soft white loaves made with white flour, milk, butter and eggs, to chewy black rye bread.

4

◀ A breadseller in Cairo, Egypt, carries ring-shaped loaves, hung on posts round his basket.

Bread may be baked in an oven or cooked in a hot pan or griddle. In some parts of the world, bread dough is steamed or deep fried. Bread comes in every shape and size, from small puffy rolls to paper-thin circles, and festival breads are sometimes baked in the shape of wheat sheaves, crescents, stars or crowns. Bread dough can also be made into cheese bread, pizza, doughnuts, crumpets and muffins.

Bread can be eaten in lots of different ways: on its own, spread with butter, margarine, jam or honey, or fried or toasted. In the Middle East and North Africa, bread is often used to mop up rich stews and sauces. Flat bread may also be spread with other foods or wrapped around fillings. We eat bread in sandwiches, burgers, hot dogs, pizzas and puddings.

How bread began

Early peoples in the Middle East were eating bread as long as 12,000 years ago. At first, they gathered wild wheat and barley grain, then they learned to farm cereal crops. Simple bread was made by mixing crushed grains with water and baking the paste on hot stones in the sun or in the ashes of fires.

By 3,000 BC, the ancient Egyptians were using sourdough to make their bread rise. They baked many different kinds of bread, using barley, millet, rye and wheat flour, sometimes adding honey, milk or eggs. The grain was ground between heavy stones and the dough was baked in clay ovens. Rich people ate the finest bread, made from flour sifted through silk to remove the grain husks.

▲ A man baking nan bread in a traditional clay oven in Dubai, in the United Arab Emirates. People have been baking flat bread like this for thousands of years.

In ancient Egypt, loaves of bread were placed in tombs to feed the dead in the afterlife.

▶ This Egyptian model showing servants making bread dates back to 1900 BC. Models like this were put in the tombs of the dead.

6

In the first century AD, the Roman Government handed out free bread to the unemployed.

▲ This bakery in Italy was built in Roman times. There is a large oven and the stone mill on the right would have been used for grinding cereal grains.

The Romans ground flour between round mill stones driven by animals or slaves. From the fourth century, they introduced watermills, which used water to turn the mill stones. They built brick bread ovens burning wood or charcoal to bake the bread. The loaves contained oil, milk, honey or cheese, flavoured with poppy, fennel and cumin seeds. The poor ate hard barley bread and the rich ate finer, white bread, dipping it in wine or goats' milk and in rich sauces.

In Britain during the Middle Ages, windmills began to be used to grind flour. Rye, barley, oats and maslin (a mix of wheat and rye) were grown, and bakeries opened in the towns and cities. People mixed dough at home and carried it to the bakery to be cooked in the bread oven. Some bakers cheated and stole the dough. If they were caught, the baker was dragged through the streets of London, with a loaf tied round their neck. Bread was sold from bakery shops and by street-sellers, who rang handbells.

Bread in the past

In the Middle Ages, food was often served on thick slices of bread, called trenchers. At the end of the meal, the trenchers were eaten, or given away to the poor. While the rich ate the finer white bread, the poor had coarse, dark bread. The poorest flour was mixed with ground peas, beans, acorns and even sawdust. Bread was eaten with fish, cheese, meat and thick stews and soups. Dried breadcrumbs were sprinkled in soups, sauces and hot milk drinks.

▼ This sixteenth-century print shows women putting loaves in the bread oven of a bakery. Some loaves would have been made with sugar, butter, eggs and spices.

A popular Medieval dish, called 'poor knights of Windsor', was made by dipping stale bread into milk and egg yolks, frying it in butter, and sprinkling it with sugar.

The word 'lord' comes from an Old English word 'hlaford' meaning 'keeper of the loaf'. Lady comes from 'hlaefdigge', which means 'kneader of the dough'.

The fashion for white bread continued until the nineteenth century, when some bakers cheated by adding alum, chalk, ground bones and even poisonous white lead to whiten their flour. This was stopped by law in 1872. By this time, wheat and other cereal crops were being grown on bigger farms, with the help of new machinery including seed drills, better ploughs, threshing machines and harvesters.

A new type of mill for grinding grain through rollers was introduced in the 1840s. At first, it was powered by steam and then by electricity. The roller mills removed all the germ and bran to make finer, whiter flour. White bread has remained popular in the twentieth century, but food scientists have proved that much of the goodness of cereals is in the bran and germ, so brown bread, made from wholemeal flour, is better for us.

◀ A London baker in Victorian times. Bread was sold from shops, baskets or hand carts.

What is in bread?

▲ Some types of flour which can be used to make bread. They are (clockwise): millet, buckwheat, medium oatmeal, gram, polenta and rye.

Bread can be made from wheat, barley, rye, maize, oat or millet flour. The different grains used help to give bread its colour, texture and flavour. Maize flour gives a crumbly yellow cornbread, barley and oats give a sweeter taste, and rye bread is dark and has a nutty flavour.

Most bread is made from wheat flour. At modern flour mills, the grain is cleaned, crushed and sifted to remove the bran and germ. These may be mixed back in to make wholewheat flour. Wholewheat flour uses the whole grain, including the bran and germ. It is a heavier, coarser flour containing more goodness. White flour is lighter and stores better.

▶ In Amazonia, Brazil, flour made from cassavas is toasted on huge griddles like this before being used to make flat bread.

When wheat flour is mixed with water, it makes a stretchy substance called gluten. The baker may add yeast to help the bread to rise. Yeast is a tiny living plant which needs warmth, moisture and food to grow. When it is mixed into bread dough, it starts to feed on the sugar and starch in the dough. As the yeast grows, it becomes frothy, giving off bubbles of carbon dioxide gas. These bubbles are trapped by the stretchy gluten and the dough stretches to twice its size.

▲ Fresh yeast (right) and dried yeast (left) can both be used for breadmaking.

▼ This girl is making bread, using her hands to knead the dough.

Bread can also be raised by sourdough, fermenting grape juice or beer froth. When the dough is baked in an oven, the heat makes the gluten firm and kills the yeast, trapping air bubbles which give the bread its texture.

Bread can be made from just flour, water and yeast but the baker may add salt for flavour and milk, eggs or butter to make the bread richer. Sugar, fruit and spices can be added, to make sweet tea breads and buns.

How bread is made

In parts of the world, including the Middle East, North Africa and some European countries, bread is still made at home in the traditional way. Flour and water are mixed together by hand, which is called kneading. Kneading helps the flour to make gluten, traps air in the dough and makes it warm, all of which help it to rise.

If raised loaves are being made, a leaven like yeast or sourdough is added and the dough is left in a warm place while the loaves rise.

▲ At a bakery in Krakow, Poland, this man is weighing dough which has been mixed by a huge machine.

▶ This French baker in Paris is marking the tops of thin French loaves called ficelles, before they are baked in the oven.

◀ A man slides loaves of flat bread into an oven on long poles at a bakery in Tangier, Morocco.

Raised bread is usually baked in an oven, but flat bread may be cooked on a hot pan or griddle, or in the ashes of an open fire.

In large plant bakeries, bread is made by machines. Computer-controlled machines weigh out the ingredients and mix them at high speed to make bread dough. Fast mixing helps the yeast to make the dough rise quickly. The dough is cut and shaped in tins which have been sprayed with cooking oil. It is then baked in the ovens. Modern gas- or oil-fired bread ovens often have shelves that turn round so that the bread cooks evenly, and in some larger plant bakeries the loaves cook on a moving belt that passes through a giant oven.

When the bread is baked, it is turned out of the tins and stacked on trays to cool. Machines slice and wrap the loaves ready to be taken to shops and supermarkets.

▼ Some types of bread are fried rather than baked. This man is frying flat bread outside a restaurant in Bangladesh.

The food in bread

▲ Wholemeal bread is brown and often has a coarser texture than white bread, which contains less fibre.

Bread is good for you. Bread flour is made from the grains of cereal plants like wheat, oats and barley. Cereal grains contain carbohydrate, protein, oil, fibre, vitamins and minerals.

Each grain has three parts: the outer skin or bran, the endosperm, which is the grain's food store, and the germ which is where a new shoot will start to grow if the grain is planted. Wholemeal flour uses the whole grain, including the bran and germ, but white flour uses only the endosperm.

Wholemeal bread is healthier because there is lots of natural goodness in the bran and germ, although some white flour has vitamins and minerals added to make it more nutritious. Plain wholemeal bread is the healthiest to eat, but all kinds of bread can form part of a balanced diet.

▶ A variety of cereal grains. Bread flour is made by grinding cereal grains. The type of grain used gives the bread its flavour and colour.

▶ Bread is a nutritious food and it can be eaten in many ways. Sandwiches like these make a quick and easy snack.

Wheat germ is rich in Vitamins B and E and minerals including calcium, phosphorus and magnesium which we need to keep us healthy. The bran contains B vitamins and minerals, and is rich in fibre, which helps us to digest food and pass it through our bodies. Bread also provides some of the Vitamin C that we need each day, and some iron, which is good for the blood.

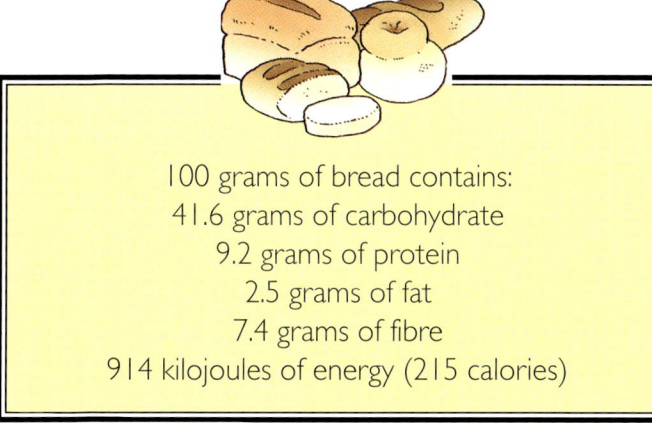

100 grams of bread contains:
41.6 grams of carbohydrate
9.2 grams of protein
2.5 grams of fat
7.4 grams of fibre
914 kilojoules of energy (215 calories)

How we eat bread

We eat bread in many different ways. It can be eaten fresh or toasted, spread with toppings such as butter, honey and jam. Toasted or fried bread can be made into croutons (small crispy cubes) which are added to soups or stews. Bread can be filled with many fillings, including meat, eggs, cheese and salad to make sandwiches. Bread buns are used to serve hot dogs and burgers.

◀ Bread is delicious served with butter and jam. In many countries, bread or toast are eaten at breakfast time.

▼ Nan breads are large, flat breads popular in India and Pakistan. People often use pieces of bread to mop up soups and curries.

Some kinds of bread, such as pitta, puff up when baked to make a pocket inside which can be filled with meat and salads. Flat breads like Mexican tortillas can be wrapped around fillings to make tacos. In China, steamed buns are filled with sweet or savoury fillings to make snacks called dim sum.

The sandwich was invented in 1762 by the Earl of Sandwich. He called for some beef to be brought to him between slices of bread, so that he could eat it while he went on gambling.

◀ At a street stall in China, this man is frying dough mixed with spinach to sell as hot, flat bread to passers-by.

In India, buns called puris are deep fried and stuffed with spicy savoury fillings to make kachori. Bread is also used to mop up stews, sauces and gravies. In France, sweet bread may be dipped into hot chocolate drinks.

▼ Summer pudding is made by putting slices of bread into a pudding basin and filling it with colourful summer berry fruits.

Breadcrumbs and beaten egg are used to make a crispy coating for fried foods such as fish or chicken. Breadcrumbs are also used to thicken soups or sauces, and are made into stuffing or bread sauce for poultry dishes.

Bread can be sweetened with sugar and dried fruits to make bread pudding, or used with soft summer fruits like redcurrants and blackcurrants to make a summer pudding.

Bread in Europe

Pizza is an Italian bread dish that dates back to Roman times. The Romans baked flat bread and topped it with oil, herbs or honey. In Italy, bread made with olive oil, such as ciabatta and focaccia, is popular. Every region has special breads, like the heart-shaped pane cuore, from Sardinia, or the carta da musica, which is a huge paper thin circle of bread, cracked like lined music paper. Grissini are crisp breadsticks, popular in Italy, Greece and Turkey.

▲ (above and right) Crumpets, hot-cross buns, tea cakes and malt loaf are a traditional part of an English afternoon tea.

◀ Italian bakers make many types of bread, like these, sometimes flavoured with fruit, nuts or seeds.

The French buy their bread fresh every day. French bread is soft and white with a crispy crust. Popular loaves are the long thin baguette (French stick) and flûte. Rich breads like brioches and croissants, made with butter, sugar and eggs, are also popular.

It is said that the French emperor Napoleon Bonaparte (1769–1821) had breadsticks sent to him daily from Italy.

In Britain, sandwich loaves baked in long rectangular tins are popular, but bread is also baked in traditional shapes like bloomers, cobs, coburgs and cottage loaves. Spiced, fruit breads are sometimes eaten for tea, along with muffins and crumpets, made with milk, butter and eggs.

The Irish enjoy soda bread, a crumbly bread made with wheat or oatmeal flour, raised with buttermilk and bicarbonate of soda.

▼ Irish soda bread like this is best eaten warm, fresh from the oven.

In Russia, Germany and parts of eastern Europe, dark breads made from rye or buckwheat flour are eaten. The Germans make pumpernickel and schwarzbrot (black bread) using rye flour. Russian blinis are pancakes, a basic form of flat bread, made from buckwheat flour.

In Austria, sweet buttery breads made with milk and eggs are popular. Ring-shaped breads made in Switzerland, Scandinavia and Iceland date back to the days when bread was baked in the autumn and stored through the winter, on poles hung from the roof beams.

Bread around the world

American cornbread was first made by the Amerindians who introduced it to the European settlers. They mixed maize flour with water and buttermilk, and baked the flat corncakes in the ashes of open fires. 'Johnny cakes' were cooked on a griddle, and contained cornmeal, wheat flour, molasses (a sugar syrup) and soured cream.

Bagels are a traditional Jewish bread, containing milk, eggs and honey or sugar. They are boiled briefly in water before baking to give a moist crumb and a glossy, chewy crust.

Mexican tortillas are made from maize flour. They may be spiced with chillie or paprika powder and wrapped around savoury fillings.

◀ Women in Oaxaca, Mexico, using a special machine to make tortillas, a flat maize bread. Tortillas are a popular snack in Mexico. They are sold at shops and stalls, and have meat or vegetable fillings.

◀ This man in Pakistan is cooking chapatis in a tandoor oven. The flat bread is pressed on to the hot sides of the clay oven, where it puffs up and turns golden.

Indian flat bread is cooked in a heavy pan called a tava, or in a clay tandoor oven. Chapatis, rotis and nan are all traditional Indian flat breads.

In the West Indies, sweet, spiced bread is popular. It contains coconut and other fruits, and is made with flour ground from maize, cassava, breadfruit or even bananas. In Jamaica, flat bread made with cassava flour is fried for breakfast.

The African flat bread injera is made from millet flour and water and is baked on a hot griddle. Some Africans make potbread by cooking dough in a pot over an open fire, and bread dough may also be rolled around a stick and then cooked over the flames.

The Chinese steam bread dough in bamboo steamers or over water in a wok (a Chinese frying pan).

▼ These baozi – Chinese bread dumplings – are being steamed in bamboo baskets over a pan of boiling water. The dumplings are sometimes filled with meat, fish or vegetables.

Bread and religion

In ancient times, bread was often baked as an offering to pagan gods or to mark special times of the year. Today, bread is still important in religious ceremonies and festivals all over the world.

In the Christian religion, bread symbolizes the body of Christ in the Holy Communion service, reminding Christians of Christ's 'last supper'. Hot-cross buns are baked at Easter and have a cross pattern on the top, to remind Christians of the cross on which Christ died. In Greece, a special plaited bread called tsoureki is baked at Easter, with a hardboiled egg dyed red on top as a symbol of new life. The Italians bake a light fruit bread called panettone in the shape of a dove at Easter, and in Germany Easter bread is baked in the shape of a hare.

▲ These Easter loaves from Turkey are decorated with red-dyed eggs, which symbolize new life.

In many European countries, spiced fruit bread is baked for Christmas, like Italian pan dolce and German stöllen, a long fruit loaf with marzipan inside, which is said to represent the Christ child in his cradle clothes.

◀ Stöllen is a fruit bread which is served at Christmas in Germany.

The Jews eat flat matzo bread for their Passover feast, recalling the time when their people fled from Egypt and did not have time to wait for the bread to rise. On the Jewish Sabbath, two special plaited loaves called challot are blessed at the table then eaten, to remind people that God gave the Jews food on their journey to the 'promised land'. Triangular buns filled with poppy seeds, called hamen tashen, are baked for the Jewish festival of Purim.

Sikhs bake chapatis for their festival of Baisakhi in April, which remembers the five friends who set up the first Sikh community. Muslims bake bread for the feast of Id-ul-Fitr, after their month of fasting called Ramadan.

▲ Sprinkling bread with salt reminds Jews of the tears shed by their people in Egypt.

▼ These women are cooking chapatis for the Sikh New Year festival of Baisakhi.

Festivals and customs

Bread may be baked to celebrate special events or times of the year. After the harvest of cereal crops, bread is a traditional part of thanksgiving or harvest festival. In Britain and other countries, harvest loaves may be baked in the shape of a wheat sheaf or crown of wheat. At Tomar in Portugal, girls take part in a harvest procession wearing tall crowns of bread decorated with ears of wheat and flowers. The bread is blessed at a church service, and the best crown is chosen before the loaves are given to the poor.

▲ Loaves shaped like sheaves of wheat are the traditional centrepiece for harvest festivals in Christian Churches.

▶ People taking part in the Festival of the Crowns of Bread at harvest time in Tomar, Portugal.

◀ This special Mexican 'bread of the dead' is placed on altars in homes and churches and on the graves of dead relations.

Mexicans bake a sweet, rich bread called pan de muertos or 'bread of the dead', for the Day of the Dead festival in November, when they remember their dead relatives.

At St. Gallen in Switzerland, there is an old custom of making bread in the shape of Altjahrmann (Old Year Man) to give to children who make lanterns for the New Year procession.

In Germany and Switzerland, gebildbrote (picture breads) are baked in decorative shapes and patterns for New Year, as well as for family occasions like weddings, births and christenings.

In Russia there is an old custom of welcoming guests with freshly baked bread and salt. The Russian world for hospitality means 'bread and salt'. Bread and salt are also traditional lucky gifts for couples getting married in Poland and Germany.

▼ These doll-like loaves have been shaped and painted to look like people. They are offered to the dead on All Souls' Day in Bolivia.

Bread recipes for you to try

Banana bread

To make a loaf of banana bread you will need:

175 g plain flour
50 g caster sugar
2 size 3 eggs, beaten
50 g soft butter
1½ teaspoons baking powder

2 large bananas, mashed with
 1½ teaspoons of lemon juice
a pinch of salt
a pinch of bicarbonate of soda

1 In a large bowl, mix together the butter and sugar with a wooden spoon. Beat in the egg, a little at a time.

2 Use a sieve to sift the flour into another bowl, and add the salt, baking powder and bicarbonate of soda, mixing them all together.

3 Beat some of the flour into the butter and sugar, then beat in some of the mashed banana and keep on adding more flour and more banana until they are really well mixed.

4 Rub some butter or margarine around a 450 g loaf tin, then spoon in the banana dough. Bake in an oven at 180° Centigrade (350° Fahrenheit, gas mark 4) for about one hour.

5 If you push a knife into your banana bread, it should come out clean when it is cooked. Let the loaf cool down in the tin for about 15 minutes, then turn it out onto a wire rack to cool.

Serve the banana bread sliced and buttered.

27

Simple chapatis

To make eight chapatis you will need:

225 g wholemeal flour   pinch of salt
25 g butter   cooking oil to just cover a heavy fry pan
175 ml water

1 Put the flour and salt into a mixing bowl. Using a knife, cut the butter into small pieces and then rub it into the flour using a pastry cutter or with your fingers.

2 Bit by bit, add the water and mix the dough together with your hands. Place the ball of dough on a pastry board with a little flour. You should knead the dough for about 15 minutes until it feels soft and stretchy.

3 To knead, fold the dough towards you on the board, then push it away with the palm of your hand. Spin it round and repeat the pulling and pushing until the dough feels stretchy.

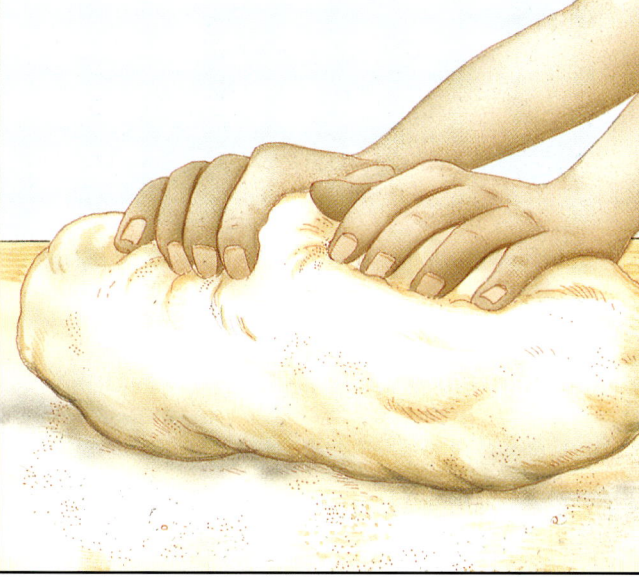

4 Leave the dough covered with a damp cloth or a plastic bag for about half an hour.

5 Divide the dough into eight pieces and shape each into a ball. Use a rolling pin to roll out each ball thin and flat.

6 Ask an adult to help you to heat a little oil in a frying pan, then take one of the chapatis and cook it for one or two minutes until bubbles appear. Use a spatula to turn it over and cook the other side for the same length of time. Repeat until all the chapatis are cooked.

Glossary

afterlife A life after death, which some religions believe takes place.
alum A mix of metals.
Amerindians American Indians, the original peoples of America.
bran The outer skin and husk of a cereal grain.
breadfruit A starchy kind of tropical fruit.
carbohydrate Starchy substances found in bread and other foods.
cassava A kind of starchy root vegetable which can be dried and ground to make flour.
cereal plants Plants whose seeds are eaten.
dough A mix of flour and water.
endosperm The white, starchy food store of a cereal grain.
fasting Going without certain or all foods, for health or religious reasons.
fermenting A chemical change which can be caused or speeded up by adding a leaven.
fibre Part of food which helps us digest food and pass it through our bodies.
germ Part of a cereal grain from which a shoot can grow.
gluten A stretchy sort of starch found in cereal plants.
griddle A circular iron plate used for cooking.
Holy Communion The Christian ceremony in which bread and wine represent the body and blood of Christ.
husk The outer skin of the grain of a cereal plant.
knead To work dough with the hands.
leaven A substance added to dough to make it rise.
Medieval From the period of the Middle Ages.
Middle Ages The time in history from the fifth to the fifteenth century.
minerals Substances found in some foods which we need to keep us healthy.
nutritious Containing goodness.
pagan Non-religious.
plant bakeries Large factory bakeries where bread is made.
protein Part of food that we need to build and repair our bodies.
Sabbath A religious day of rest – Sunday in the Christian religion, Saturday in the Jewish religion.
seed drills Farm machinery for planting seeds.
sourdough Dough allowed to ferment which is used as a leaven.
starch A kind of carbohydrate.
tandoor A kind of domed clay oven used in India

threshing machine Farm machinery for separating cereal grain from the stalks.

unleavened Flat bread that does not contain a leaven.

vitamins Substances found in some foods which we need to keep us healthy.

wheat sheaves Bundles of wheat.

white bread Bread that is made from white flour, which has had the bran removed.

wholemeal bread Bread that is made from wholemeal flour, which contains the whole cereal grain, including the bran.

yeast A live plant which makes dough rise.

Books to read

All About Bread by Geoffrey Patterson (Andre Deutsch, 1984)

Bread by Judith Baskerville (A & C Black, 1987)

Bread by Dorothy Turner (Wayland, 1988)

Making Bread by Ruth Thomson (Franklin Watts, 1986)

For further information about bread, contact:

The Flour Advisory Bureau
21 Arlington Street
London
SW1A 1RN

Index

Numbers in **bold** show subjects that appear in pictures.

Africa 21
Amazonia **4, 10**
Amerindians 20
Austria 19

bagels 20
Bangladesh **13**
baozi **21**
blinis 19
Bolivia **25**
Bonaparte, Napoleon 18
Brazil **4, 10**
bread pudding 17
brioches 18

carbohydrates 14
cassava flour **4**, 4, **10**, 10, 21
challot 23
chapatis **4, 21**, 21, **23**
China 16, **17, 21**, 21
cornbread 10
corncakes 20
croissants 18
crumpets **4**, 5, **18**, 19

dim sum 16
doughnuts 5

Egypt 4, 6

festivals 4, 5, 22–3, 24–5
France **12**, 17

French breads **4, 12**, 18
Germany 19, 22, 25
gluten 11, 12
gram flour 10
Greece 22

hamen tashen 23
hot-cross buns **18**, 22

Iceland 19
India 4, 16, 17, 21
injera 21
Israel **1**
Italian breads **18**, 18, 22
Italy 7, 18, 22

Jamaica 2

kachori 17

malt loaf **18**
matzo bread 23
Mexico 4, 20, **25**, 25
Middle Ages 7, 8
Middle East 4, 5, 6, 12
mills 7, 9, 10
minerals 14, 15
Morocco **13**
muffins 5, 19

nan **4, 6, 16**
North Africa 5, 12

Pakistan 16, **22**
pitta bread **4**, 16
pizza 5, 18
Poland **12**, 25
Portugal **24**, 24

pot bread 21
protein 14
pumpernickel 19
puris 17

recipes
    banana bread 26–7
    simple chapatis 28–9
religion 20, **22–25**, 22–3, 24
Romans 7, 18
Russia 19, 25
rye bread **4**, 4

Sandwich, Earl of 17
sandwiches 5, **15**, 16, 17, 19
Sardinia 18
Scandinavia 19
schwarzbrot 19
soda bread **4, 19**, 19
stöllen **22**, 22
summer pudding **17**, 17
Switzerland 19, 25

tea cakes **18**
tortillas **4**, 16, **20**, 20
tsoureki 22
Turkey 18, 22

United Arab Emirates **6**
USA 4

vitamins 14, 15

West Indies 21

yeast 4, **11**, 11, 13

32